Where Is Illinois?

Where Is Illinois?

by Tracy Vonder Brink

illustrated by Ted Hammond

Penguin Workshop

For my grandparents, parents,
and all my Illinois family—TVB

PENGUIN WORKSHOP
An imprint of Penguin Random House LLC
1745 Broadway, New York, NY 10019
penguinrandomhouse.com

Designed and Produced by Dinardo Design, LLC.

Library of Congress Cataloging-in-Publication Data is available.

First published in the United States of America by Penguin Workshop, 2025

Manufactured in the United States of America
CJKW

ISBN 9798217051465 (paperback)
10 9 8 7 6 5 4 3 2 1

ISBN 9798217051472 (library binding)
10 9 8 7 6 5 4 3 2 1

The authorized representative in the EU for product safety and compliance is Penguin Random House Ireland, Morrison Chambers, 32 Nassau Street, Dublin D02 YH68, Ireland, https://eu-contact.penguin.ie.

Contents

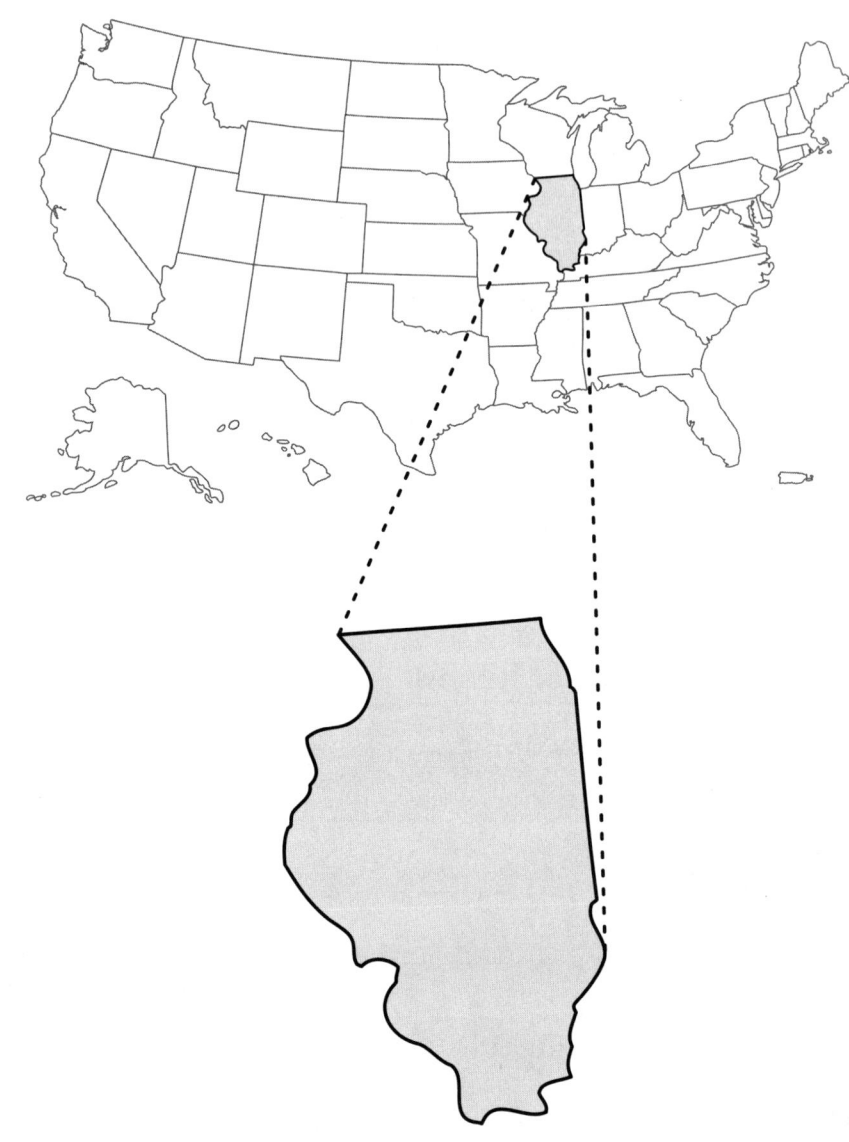

Where Is Illinois?

In 1854, Abraham Lincoln stood in front of a crowd gathered on the Peoria, Illinois, courthouse lawn. Lincoln had once been a member of the Illinois House of Representatives, but he hadn't held office in five years. He'd come to Peoria to speak out against a bill that would allow slavery in Nebraska, a new territory.

Lincoln told the crowd that slavery was a "monstrous injustice" and said it was wrong for one person to enslave another. He reminded people that the Declaration of Independence said all men are created equal and have rights. By the end of his three-hour speech, Lincoln had made a powerful argument against slavery.

One hundred and fifty years later, Barack Obama stood in front of a crowd at the Democratic

National Convention. He'd been asked to give the keynote address, the main speech at the gathering. He was an Illinois state senator, but few people outside the state had heard of him.

Obama told the crowd about his family. He talked about his parents' dreams for him. He told the people listening to him that America was a great nation because the Declaration of Independence said all men are created equal and have rights. By the end of his seventeen-minute speech, Obama proved he was a powerful speaker.

Lincoln's Peoria speech and Obama's keynote address were turning points in their careers. Their strong public speaking set them on the path to the White House and would eventually convince the people of the United States to elect them president—and make them two of Illinois's most famous residents.

CHAPTER 1
Welcome to Illinois

Illinois has a rich history that stretches back thousands of years. Its farmers grow crops and raise animals that feed millions. It's home to the city of Chicago. Presidents, inventors, musicians, and many notable people have all called this state home.

Illinois's total land area is 57,918 square miles, making it the twenty-fourth-largest US state. More than eight hundred miles of rivers form the state's boundaries. It also has sixty-three miles of shoreline along Lake Michigan, one of the Great Lakes. The Ohio River divides Illinois from Kentucky, and the Wabash River separates the state from Indiana. Illinois also neighbors Wisconsin.

The Mississippi River, the state's longest, separates it from Iowa and Missouri. Kaskaskia (say: ka-ska-SKEE-uh) Island is the only Illinois town separated from the state by water—it's surrounded by the Mississippi River! Flooding more than one hundred years ago changed where the river ran and cut Kaskaskia off from the rest of Illinois.

Floods still cause big problems in the state. Central Illinois has about fifty days of storms each year. When the rain is heavy, rivers overflow, harming homes and crops. Flooding sometimes causes billions of dollars of damage in a single year, and flood losses in Illinois are the third highest of any state in the country.

Thunderstorms bring about half of Illinois's rain, most often in the spring and summer. Summers are hot, with the temperatures reaching into the nineties. In winter, it's often as cold as twenty degrees Fahrenheit—or even colder. The northern parts of the state are cooler. Northern Illinois has up to thirty-six inches of snow every year, but it snows less than ten inches in the south.

Illinois's climate hasn't always been the same as it is today. About three hundred million years ago, steamy swamps covered much of southern Illinois. They were filled with plants like trees and giant ferns. As these plants died, they sank to the bottom of the swamps. Over millions of years, bits of rocks and minerals called sediment piled up, pressed down, and turned the layers underneath them into coal. Thanks to its ancient swamps, Illinois has some of the largest amounts of coal in the United States. There may be as many as two hundred billion tons of coal underground.

Glaciers (large bodies of ice that stay frozen for hundreds or even thousands of years) played a big role in creating the state's landforms. They covered almost all of Illinois at least once during the Pleistocene Epoch (say: ply-sto-seen ep-ock),

2.6 million to ten thousand years ago. The ice was about two thousand feet thick in some places! As the glaciers' heavy weight caused them to slide forward, they flattened the land. Thanks to the glaciers, about 85 percent of the state is flat. Only some areas in northwestern and southern Illinois escaped the ice.

As the glaciers moved, they picked up soil and rocks and ground them into sediment. When the ice melted, it left the sediment behind, and wind spread it around. Sediment carried and dropped by wind is called loess (say: LUSS). Loess holds water and is full of nutrients—making Illinois perfect for farming.

Glaciers also helped create the Mississippi River, which became an important resource. Some of the first Indigenous people in Illinois lived in the area around the Mississippi River between 900 and 1200 CE. Because their way of life developed around the river, we call them the

Mississippians. We don't know what they called themselves, and they were probably made up of many nations.

One of the major Mississippian settlements can still be seen today at Cahokia (say: kuh-HOH-kee-uh) Mounds in southwestern Illinois.

The city had over one hundred mounds, and more than ten thousand people may have lived there. Buildings might have topped some of the mounds. Other mounds were used for burials. Monks Mound is one hundred feet tall and is the largest human-made mound in the United States. More than two thousand other Mississippian sites have been found throughout Illinois.

After four hundred years, the Mississippian civilization fell apart. We don't know why they abandoned their cities and villages. They were gone by the 1500s. That's when the Inoka, an alliance of Indigenous people that included the Kaskaskia and the Peoria peoples, left southern Michigan and moved to what is today Illinois.

The Ojibwa (say: oh-JIB-way), a people from north of the Great Lakes region, used the word *Illini* for the Inoka people. French explorers who came to the area in the 1600s had their own version of the word *Illini*—Illinois! At that time,

France controlled an area that stretched from Canada to what is now Louisiana. That included all the land around the Mississippi River.

The governor of this area—called New France—asked two men to explore the river. Jacques Marquette was a Jesuit missionary (a person sent by the Catholic Church to teach about their religion). He learned some of the Indigenous languages. Louis Jolliet was a French Canadian fur trader and explorer. The two of them began their journey in May 1673. They traveled in two canoes with five other men.

As they paddled down the Mississippi, they saw swans, geese, and huge fish. They watched deer and turkeys in the forests along the riverbanks. They also visited villages built by the Peoria and Kaskaskia peoples. One of the Kaskaskia settlements they saw may have had as many as fifteen hundred people living there.

Marquette and Jolliet's trip covered two

thousand miles. The reports they made about the
land and people they saw convinced the French
government to set up trading posts along the river.
In 1699, Cahokia became the first permanent
French settlement near the Mississippi River.
In the 1700s, the French built more villages in
Illinois, including Kaskaskia, which was named
after the Indigenous people.

In 1754, France went to war with Great Britain. The French lost and had to give up the region they called the Illinois Country. The British didn't hold it for long, though. Soon, the American colonies were ready to fight for their independence.

CHAPTER 2
The Path to Statehood

The American Revolution began in 1775. Most of it was fought far from Illinois. Colonel George Rogers Clark volunteered to lead Americans against British forts. In 1778, Clark and 175 soldiers headed to Kaskaskia. They arrived on July 4 and discovered the British had left—the fort was only guarded by one man!

Clark went on to capture other British forts and towns in Illinois. Because he was from Virginia, the Illinois Country became part of Virginia's territory—even though there were already people living there, such as settler Jean Baptiste Pointe DuSable.

Jean Baptiste Pointe DuSable
(before 1750–1818)

Jean Baptiste Pointe DuSable may have been born in Haiti. His mother was an enslaved African woman and his father a French sailor. Not much is known about DuSable's early life, including the exact year he was born. It's thought he traveled to France with his father and received some education there.

In 1765, DuSable arrived in New Orleans in the United States and became a trader. He traveled and learned Indigenous languages. In 1778, he married a Potawatomi (say: po-tuh-WA-tuh-me) woman named Kitihawa. Marrying Kitihawa made DuSable part of the Potawatomi community. DuSable and Kitihawa settled on the banks of what is now the Chicago River near Lake Michigan. They lived in a small cabin and ran a farm and busy trading post that had a bakehouse, workshop, and more. They also had two children.

In 1800, DuSable sold his land and moved to Peoria. Today, he's remembered as the first non-Indigenous person to settle what is now the Chicago area. In 2021, Chicago's famous Lake Shore Drive was renamed in his honor.

Virginia had claimed Illinois but soon found it too large to look after. It was turned over to the US government in 1784. The Illinois Country became part of the Northwest Territory, the land north and west of the Ohio River. Arthur St. Clair was the Northwest Territory's first governor. In 1790, he created Illinois's first county (a part of a state that has its own local government). He named it after himself—St. Clair County.

Slavery was banned in the Northwest Territory. When Illinois joined, some of its settlers already enslaved people. St. Clair decided that anyone who was already enslaved in Illinois would not be freed, but no more enslaved people could be brought into the territory. In 1807, the territorial government passed a law that said enslavers could make "contracts" that kept people as workers and servants. Some of the contracts lasted as long as ninety-nine years, and the enslaved people were forced to sign them, so it was still a form of slavery. Enslaved Black and Indigenous people were forced to keep working in Illinois homes, farms, and mines.

More and more people were moving to the Northwest Territory, although far fewer lived in Illinois than in the rest. As settlers pushed into the territory, they took land from Indigenous people. Indigenous leaders had no choice but to sign peace agreements that gave up their land in parts of the Northwest Territory. In Illinois, a peace agreement granted the US government land at the mouth of the Chicago River.

The US government made millions of acres of Illinois land available for white settlers to buy at low prices. Settlers who moved from the eastern parts of the United States had never seen anything like the prairie grasses and colorful wildflowers that covered Illinois. In some places, the grass grew ten feet tall! The way it rippled in the wind reminded them of ocean waves, so the prairie was

sometimes called a sea of grass. Illinois became known as the Prairie State and had twenty-two million acres of prairie. Later, almost all of the prairie would be turned into farmland.

In 1818, the people of Illinois asked Congress to make Illinois a state. Congress said yes, and Illinois became the twenty-first state. Its northern boundary was moved up 8,500 miles to touch Lake Michigan. Illinois's first constitution banned

slavery—except it allowed enslaver "contracts" to continue and didn't free any people who were already enslaved. Later, another law banned free Black people from moving to the state. Free Black people who already lived there had to carry papers to prove it. Not everyone in Illinois agreed with slavery or the harsh laws against free Black Americans, but they didn't yet have the power to change it.

CHAPTER 3
From Settlers to Skyscrapers

In the early 1800s, American settlers in northwestern and southern Illinois realized some of the ground held lead (say: LED). Lead is a metal that could be used to make water pipes, household goods like cups and plates, and much more. People rushed to the area, hoping to strike it rich. Galena—named after the Latin word for lead—was settled as a mining town. Millions of pounds of Galena lead would be shipped down the Mississippi River.

Illinois lead might have been a discovery for the American settlers, but it wasn't new to the area's Indigenous people. More than a thousand years earlier, the Mississippians dug for it. Long before Illinois became a state, the Sac and the

Fox people mined lead there. In 1822, hundreds of American miners pushed into lands claimed by the Sac and the Fox. Sac and Fox leaders asked the US government to stop them, but the government refused. Then, while Sac and Fox people were away on a hunt, settlers took over their villages. The US government also put Sac and Fox lands up for sale, forcing them to move across the Mississippi River.

In 1832, a Sac leader named Black Hawk brought a group of about one thousand Sac, Fox, and Kickapoo people into Illinois. Black Hawk and his followers wanted to settle peacefully, but the governor of Illinois thought they were there to make war. He asked the US Army for help. He also sent out the militia (local people who sometimes acted as soldiers). The militia attacked, and Black Hawk and his men fought back. The Black Hawk War began.

Some Kickapoo, Potawatomi, and Winnebago

people joined Black Hawk, but they couldn't defeat the US Army and the Illinois militia. Most of Black Hawk's people were killed or died trying to escape the fighting. After the Black Hawk War, the US government forced all Indigenous nations in Illinois to sign treaties to give up their land and leave the state, even those who hadn't joined Black Hawk. Forcing the Indigenous people to leave led to even more American settlement in Illinois.

Mining became a booming business. Immigrants from Great Britain and Europe, including places like Ireland and Italy, worked in Illinois mines digging coal, which was used as a fuel to power factories, heat homes, and more. By the mid-1800s, one million tons of coal had been mined in Illinois. A railroad was built in Chicago, which helped transport the coal.

Trains also helped move goods being farmed in Illinois. A blacksmith from Vermont, John

Deere, had moved to Illinois along with many others seeking land and jobs. After seeing farmers struggle with iron plows that got stuck in the sticky prairie soil, he invented a steel plow with a more polished surface that would move through the sticky soil more easily. Soon, he was making one thousand plows a year to sell to local farmers!

Inventor Cyrus McCormick opened a factory in Chicago where he made harvesting machines. Like John Deere's plow, these inventions made farming faster and easier. By the 1840s, German farmers were flocking to northeastern Illinois. They settled Arlington Heights, Calumet City, Carol Stream, and more.

The town of Galesburg was founded with the idea of establishing a college there (Knox College). The townspeople were against slavery and felt very strongly it should be outlawed. They formed the Illinois Anti-Slavery Society there in 1837. More anti-slavery groups followed, and within the next year, there were twelve others across the state. These groups held public meetings, gave speeches, and wrote newspaper articles calling for the end of slavery. Later, they worked to have anti-slavery candidates elected so that the laws could be changed. Illinois was also part of the Underground Railroad, the network of safe houses and secret routes that helped enslaved Black people reach safety in the North. Thousands of freedom seekers were guided through the state.

John Jones, a wealthy free Black businessman who lived in Chicago, used his home as a stop on the Underground Railroad. He and his wife Mary helped hundreds of freedom seekers escape. Jones also led a movement against slavery and the laws that limited the rights of free Black people. Later, he became the first Black elected official in Chicago.

After Abraham Lincoln's Peoria speech, newspapers wrote about him, and he became well-known in Illinois. This helped him build a new career in politics. In the 1860 presidential election, he ran against Stephen A. Douglas and two other candidates. The United States was torn between those who wanted to ban slavery and those who wanted to keep it. Lincoln didn't win any of the Southern states, but he had

enough votes to be elected president. Southern states didn't want a president who was against slavery, so they left the United States to form their own country, called the Confederate States of America.

The Civil War began in 1861. No Civil War battles were fought in Illinois, but more than two hundred thousand Illinoisans fought on the side of the US government (also called the Union), including one regiment of free Black men from Quincy. In 1865, Illinois was the first state to approve the Thirteenth Amendment, which banned slavery in all forms throughout the United States. The state also removed the law that had said no free Black people could move there.

After the Civil War ended, the United States built railroads that stretched to California. Chicago was located between the East and West Coasts. The city's location near farmlands made it easy for farmers to bring their crops to market. Farmers also sold animals there. Chicago became the country's largest meatpacking center after the Union Stockyards, filled with pens for cows, sheep, and pigs, opened on the city's South Side. Thousands of workers at Philip Armour's factory packed millions of dollars' worth of pork and beef every year.

Other kinds of industry (businesses that change raw materials into goods) also grew in Illinois after the Civil War. The number of factories in the state more than doubled in just ten years! By 1870, Illinois's population was over two million, with close to three hundred thousand people living in Chicago.

In the fall of 1871, tragedy struck Chicago. It had barely rained in months, and a hot wind blew. Nearly everything in the city was made of

wood—even the sidewalks. On the evening of October 8, fire broke out in a barn on Chicago's West Side. The flames quickly spread north and east, into the city's center. By the time firefighters arrived, the fire raged out of control. It even jumped into the Chicago River, where oil and waste that polluted the water caught fire. When rain finally put it out, the fire had destroyed more than seventeen thousand buildings and seventy-three miles of streets. Ninety thousand people

lost their homes, and it's thought that several hundred died. The Great Chicago Fire was one of the worst disasters in US history.

After the fire, a new city rose from the ashes. Not everyone could afford to rebuild. Local laws were changed to require fireproof brick, stone, and marble be used, but these materials were too expensive for most small shops. Chicago's big businesses could afford it, though, and their buildings changed the look of the city.

Marshall Field was a businessman who opened a six-story department store on State Street. His store launched one of Chicago's busiest shopping areas. The Home Insurance Building was made with a steel frame and was ten stories high. Lighter-weight steel frames meant buildings could be taller because steel weighed less than wood and stone. The Home Insurance Building seemed so tall it was called a "skyscraper"—one of the world's first!

Chicago became a city of firsts. Softball was invented there in 1887: Reporter George Hancock saw someone toss and hit a boxing glove with a broom handle and quickly made up rules for a new sport. In 1893, the Chicago World's Fair, which ran for six months and included displays from forty-six countries, featured the world's first Ferris wheel. That same year, Daniel Hale Williams performed the world's first heart surgery at Provident Hospital, the country's first Black-owned hospital.

The city was also a center for science. In 1900, engineers (people trained to use math and science to solve problems) changed the Chicago River to flow backward so the city would have clean water. The Museum of Science and Industry opened. The University of Chicago brought experts from around the world to work in its eight science buildings. Years later, the university would be the home of the world's first nuclear reactor, a machine that splits atoms (the very small building blocks that make up everything in the universe) to release energy.

As Chicago grew, farming remained important to the rest of Illinois. Farm life was changing. After John Deere bought a company that made gasoline-powered tractors in 1918, farmers stopped using horse-pulled plows. The new machines meant more crops could be raised with less work. Scientists at the University of Illinois at Urbana-Champaign (say: urr-BA-nuh SHAM-payn) studied soybeans—a crop that came to the United States from Japan—and introduced them to farmers. By the 1920s, Illinois grew more soybeans than any other state.

More farming machines meant fewer people were needed to work the land. More and more young people left to take jobs in cities. The state's cities also grew as thousands of Black Americans left the South and moved north. Spanish-speaking

Bo Diddley performing

people also came to Illinois, like those from Mexico and Puerto Rico. These communities brought their culture with them and helped make Chicago and other Illinois cities centers for music and art.

In the 1920s and '30s, blues and jazz shaped American music. Black Chicagoans like Duke Ellington, Louis Armstrong, Nat King Cole, and Muddy Waters helped invent these new kinds of music. Blues and jazz also led to other styles of music such as big band in the 1940s and rock and roll music in the 1950s. Bo Diddley, the legendary guitar player who helped invent the rock and roll sound, recorded his music at Chicago's Chess Records. So did Aretha Franklin, the Rolling Stones, and many more!

From music to science and many fields in between, Illinois helped build the world we live in today.

Reversing the Chicago River

Chicago faced a big problem in the 1800s. Its water was making people sick. Every day, factories and city pipes poured waste into the Chicago River. The river then carried the pollution into Lake Michigan. The lake was supposed to supply the city with clean drinking water, but the dirty river made the lake water unsafe. In 1854, more than fourteen hundred people died from sickness caused by bad water. Chicagoans demanded something be done.

The city turned to Ellis Sylvester Chesbrough (say: CHESS-bro), who had been in charge of building Boston's water supply. Chesbrough came up with a bold plan—change the direction the river flowed! The dirty water would move away from Lake Michigan and toward the Mississippi River. The lake's water would be safe to drink again. (Ways to clean wastewater hadn't been invented yet.)

To change the river, the city needed to build a twenty-eight-mile canal (a really big ditch) that ran downhill and connected the river to the Des Plaines River, which drained away from the lake. They put in a dam to hold back the Chicago River while they worked. When the canal was finished, the dam was removed. The river ran downhill into the canal. That made it pull water from Lake Michigan and flow away from the lake.

Reversing the Chicago River wasn't easy. It took fifteen thousand people eight years of hard work. They used explosives, steam shovels, and wagons pulled by horses and mules to remove more than forty-two million cubic yards of rock and soil. Today, it's remembered as one of the world's greatest building projects.

CHAPTER 4
The Great State of Illinois

More than twelve million people now live in Illinois. Around one million make their homes in rural areas. Chicago is the biggest city in Illinois—the city and the area around it have a population of more than nine million people! It's the third-largest city in the United States by population. Other Illinois cities include Aurora, Joliet, and Naperville.

Fewer people may live in the countryside, but the state's more than seventy thousand farms earn about $50 billion each year. Almost all are owned by families. Illinois leads the United States in producing soybeans and is a top producer of corn and pigs. It also grows more pumpkins than any other state. Morton is known as the Pumpkin

Capital of the World because 85 percent of the world's pumpkin is canned there!

Visitors to Illinois will spot tall wind turbines in some of the state's fields. The blades on these machines spin to catch the wind and turn it into electricity. Illinois has more than three thousand wind turbines and plans to build more. The state's wind farms make enough electricity to power two million homes every year.

The state's food industry turns farmers' crops and meat into many products. Chicago has more than two thousand of these food-manufacturing companies. Quaker Oats, Oscar Mayer, and Keebler are all based there. So is Nabisco, which owns the world's largest bakery! The city is also home to some "Chicago-style" twists on popular foods, such as deep-dish pizza and Chicago dogs—100 percent pure beef hot dogs with yellow mustard, sweet relish, chopped onions, tomatoes, and other toppings.

Illinois has continued to be a leader in science. The cell phone was invented there! At Fermi National Accelerator Laboratory, also known as Fermilab, scientists use powerful machines to study physics, a field of science that helps us understand the universe. Chicago's Field Museum of Natural History has a collection of more than twenty-four million objects, including Sue, the

largest and most complete *Tyrannosaurus rex* skeleton to be discovered so far.

The city is the home of Major League Baseball teams the Cubs and the White Sox. The Cubs play at Wrigley Field, the second-oldest baseball stadium in the United States. Chicago also has one of the oldest teams in the National Football League—the Chicago Bears. The Bears played their first game in 1920, before the National Football League was formed in 1922. Basketball great Michael Jordan lived in Illinois for nineteen years and led the Chicago Bulls to six National Basketball Association championships.

Another famous Chicagoan named Michelle Robinson was working as a lawyer when Barack Obama took a summer job with her law firm in 1989. Three years later, they married. Michelle became first lady when Barack was elected the president of the United States in 2008. President Ronald Reagan also grew up in Illinois, and visitors can tour his family home in Dixon.

Abraham Lincoln's Presidential Library and Museum is in Springfield, along with his home. The National Park Service takes care of Lincoln's home and other important sites in Illinois. The US Forest Service looks after Shawnee National Forest, where hikers enjoy the Garden of the Gods, which has rock formations that are millions

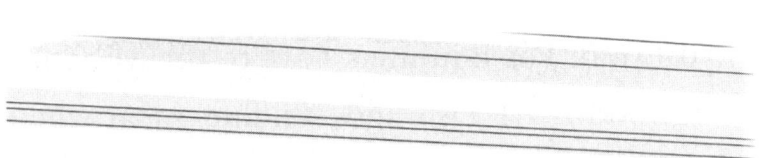

of years old. Fossil hunters head to the Mazonia-Braidwood State Fish and Wildlife Area, where they can search for the state fossil, known as the Tully Monster. This slug-like sea creature had a long toothy snout, but scientists still don't know exactly what it was!

Cahokia Mounds, the former city of the Mississippians, is an important historic site. Illinois is also working to recognize the Indigenous people who live there today. The Prairie Band Potawatomi Nation led a movement to have some of its land returned. A treaty made in 1829 had given 1,500 acres of land in Illinois to the leader of the nation and his people, but the United States sold the land to white settlers instead. In 2024, the United States government agreed that the land rightfully belonged to the Prairie Band Potawatomi Nation and transferred ownership of a 1,500-acre state park west of Chicago to them. Prairie Band Potawatomi is the first Indigenous nation in Illinois to be officially recognized by the government.

From ancient Cahokia to modern Chicago, Illinois is home to important cities. Its farms and factories help feed the world. Its people have been dreamers and makers. When talking about Illinois, Abraham Lincoln might have said it best: "To this place, and the kindness of these people, I owe everything."

Illinois at a Glance

Statehood: 1818

Nickname: The Prairie State

Abbreviation: IL

State Motto: State Sovereignty, National Union

State Tree: White oak

State Animal: White-tailed deer

Capital: Springfield

Size: 57,918 square miles

Population: Over 12 million

Famous People from Illinois:

Hillary Clinton (former first lady), Harrison Ford (actor), Carl Sandburg (poet), Jackie Joyner-Kersee (Olympic athlete), Jennifer Hudson (singer/actor)

State flag

State flower
Violet

State bird
Northern cardinal

FUN FACT:
Popcorn is Illinois's state snack.
"Chicago-style" popcorn is a mix
of cheese and caramel popcorn.

Timeline of Illinois

900–1200	Monks Mound, the largest human-made mound in North America, is built by the Mississippians
1673	Explorers Jacques Marquette and Louis Jolliet travel down the Mississippi River
1787	The Illinois Country is part of the Northwest Territory
1818	Illinois becomes the twenty-first US state
1832	The Black Hawk War ends, and Indigenous nations are forced to give up their land and leave the state
1860	Abraham Lincoln is elected president
1865	Illinois is the first state to approve the Thirteenth Amendment to ban slavery
1871	The Great Chicago Fire burns more than seventeen thousand buildings
1900	Engineers permanently reverse the flow of the Chicago River
1955	Bo Diddley releases his debut single, "Bo Diddley"
2008	Barack Obama is elected president
2024	The US government returns land to the Prairie Band Potawatomi Nation

Timeline of the World

1176	The London Bridge is built in England
1620	Pilgrims from England land at Plymouth Rock
1780	The Great Hurricane hits the Caribbean and becomes the Atlantic Ocean's deadliest known hurricane
1818	English author Mary Shelley publishes *Frankenstein*
1832	Greece wins its independence from the Ottoman Empire
1854	Trade opens between Japan and the United States
1863	The Red Cross is founded in Switzerland
1872	Yellowstone becomes the world's first national park
1889	The Eiffel Tower opens in Paris
1898	Spain declares war on the United States, starting the Spanish-American War
1901	Australia becomes a nation
1939	World War II begins
1963	Martin Luther King Jr. gives his "I Have a Dream" speech
2005	YouTube is launched
2024	The thirty-third Summer Olympic Games are held in Paris

Bibliography

*Books for young readers

*Anderson, Kirsten. *Who Is Michael Jordan?* New York: Penguin Workshop, 2019.

*Burgen, Michael. *Illinois*. America the Beautiful. Third Series. New York: Scholastic Inc., 2014.

"Cahokia Mounds." *Britannica Kids*. kids.britannica.com/kids/article/Cahokia-Mounds/629742.

*Edwards, L.C. *Illinois*. Minneapolis: Abdo Publishing, 2023.

*Edwards, Roberta. *Who Is Barack Obama?* New York: Penguin Workshop, 2009.

"Event Timeline." *Illinois Department of Natural Resources: Historic Preservation Division*. dnrhistoric.illinois.gov/research/sitepages/timeline.html.

"Fun Facts." *Illinois.gov*. www.illinois.gov/about/fun-facts.html.

"Illinois." *Britannica Kids*. kids.britannica.com/kids/article/Illinois/345481.

"Illinois." *National Geographic Kids*. kids.nationalgeographic.com/geography/states/article/ illinois.

*Pascal, Janet B. *Who Was Abraham Lincoln?* New York: Penguin Workshop, 2008.